Written by
Celia Bland

Illustrated by
Tony Tallarico

Kidsbooks®

Visit us at www.kidsbooks.com®

What is the Bible?

The Bible is not just one book, but actually 66 different books. In fact, the word *Bible* comes from the Greek word *biblia*, which means "books." But all of the books have the same purpose—to tell people about God and His love for mankind. The Bible forms the basis for Judaism and Christianity. The Jewish, or Hebrew, Bible consists of the Old Testament; the Christian Bible consists of the Old and the New Testaments.

How old is the Bible?

The first books of the Bible were written on scrolls about 1,600 years before Jesus Christ was born. The Bible probably took longer to complete than any other book. The last book of the Bible, Revelation, was not finished until 60 years after the death of Christ—nearly 1,700 years later!

Who wrote the Bible?

Some 40 different men wrote the books that make up the Bible, but the Bible claims that it is the word of God, not of man. It says that God put His words into the minds of holy men, who then wrote them down.

How is the Bible organized?

The Bible is divided into two main sections: the Old Testament and the New Testament. For the most part, the books in the Bible appear chronologically—in the order in which they happened. Each book is divided into chapters, and each chapter is divided into verses.

What is the Old Testament?

The Old Testament is the first section of the Bible. It describes how the world was made and tells the history of the Jewish people. It is made up of 39 books, most of which were originally written in Hebrew.

The first 17 books of the Old Testament are called the Historical Books. They include Genesis, Exodus, Leviticus, Numbers, and Deuteronomy, which were written by Moses. After the 17 Historical Books come the five Poetical Books, beginning with the Book of Job. One of them, the Book of Psalms, is said to have been written, at least in part, by King David. The Poetical Books are followed by five books called the Major Prophets, and then 12 books called the Minor Prophets, which are the last in the Old Testament. The books of the Minor Prophets describe hardships that the Jewish people experienced as captives of other nations, but they also relate many lessons about morality and responsibility.

In the Beginning . . .

How many days did God take to create the world?

Six days. First, He created light and darkness, the heavens and sun and stars, and all of Earth's plants and animals. From the dust of the earth, God created man and named him Adam. Then He planted a garden in Eden and placed Adam there. God rested on the seventh day, called the sabbath, which means "to stop."

Who was God's final creation?

Eve. Adam was lonely in the Garden of Eden, so God took one of Adam's ribs and made a woman, who became Adam's wife.

What did God tell Adam and Eve not to do?

Eat fruit from the Tree of Knowledge of Good and Evil, which God had planted at the center of the Garden of Eden. It held the understanding of all things, good and evil. God told Adam and Eve that if they ate fruit from it, they would die.

What happened when Adam and Eve ate the fruit?

A serpent told Eve, "The fruit from the Tree of Knowledge won't really kill you. If you eat it, you will be wise like God, knowing right from wrong." Eve took a bite of the fruit, and then gave some to Adam to eat. Immediately, their eyes were opened, and they tried to hide their nakedness with fig leaves. God, who was saddened by their disobedience, made them leave the Garden of Eden. Outside Eden, they would have to work hard for their food. They would also feel pain and suffering and eventually die.

How did God punish the serpent?

For tempting Eve to do wrong, the serpent had to crawl on its belly. God told the serpent, "You will eat dust all of your life."

Brother Against Brother

WHO WERE CAIN AND ABEL?

They were the sons of Adam and Eve. They were born after Adam and Eve left Eden, and they grew up on their parents' farm.

WHY DID CAIN KILL HIS BROTHER?

Abel was a shepherd and Cain was a farmer. When the young men worshipped God, they burned offerings of Abel's lambs and Cain's fruits. God was pleased with Abel's offering, but He was not pleased with Cain's. This made Cain so jealous that he killed Abel.

WHAT DID CAIN SAY WHEN GOD ASKED HIM WHERE ABEL WAS?

"I do not know. Am I my brother's keeper?" But God knew what Cain had done. He made Cain leave his parents' land and go to the Land of Nod. To protect him, God put a mark on Cain's forehead to warn people that they would suffer a terrible punishment if they killed Cain.

Why did God flood the Earth?

God was upset by the world's wickedness. "I will destroy humans and all the other creatures," He proclaimed. But there was one man God loved. His name was Noah. God commanded Noah to build an ark and fill it with his family and a male and female of all the creatures on Earth. Noah built his 450-foot-long ark out of wood from cypress trees. He then command-ed the animals to enter two by two.

I'VE NEVER BEEN ON AN ARK BEFORE.

HOPE I WON'T GET THIRSTY!

ARE WE THERE YET?

How long did it rain?

For 40 days and 40 nights, rain flooded the Earth. Then, for the next 150 days, the floods washed over even the highest mountain peaks. It took another 150 days for the water to begin to recede. In all, Noah spent more than a year on the ark.

What was the first creature to leave the ark?

After the floods receded, Noah sent out a raven to search for land. The raven flew about and returned. Then, seven days later, Noah sent out a dove, but the dove returned. In another seven days, Noah sent the dove again. This time, the dove returned carrying an olive branch. Seven days later, Noah sent out the dove a third time, but it did not return, because it had found a place to nest.

Why did God send a rainbow?

The rainbow was a sign that promised He would never again try to destroy the world by flood.

The Tower of Babel

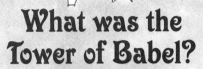

What was the Tower of Babel?

A tower that was meant to reach up into heaven. The people were no longer humble, and they were thinking more about fame and power and less about God. God knew that the people would become even more sinful if the tower were finished.

How did God stop the tower from being built?

He confused the builders by causing them to speak different languages. No one could understand anyone else, so it became impossible to finish the tower. They all moved to other lands, traveling in groups according to language. The unfinished tower eventually crumbled.

Why was this tower remembered as Babel?

The tower builders became frustrated when they could not understand each other, and referred to the languages that they could not understand as "babel." This term, with a different spelling (babble), means "a confusion of sounds."

The Patience of Job

Who was Job?

Job was a good man who loved God. He had 10 children, prosperous fields of grains and vegetables, and thousands of animals.

Why did God allow Satan to torment Job?

Satan told God that Job was not really good. "If you take away his riches, he will curse you," the devil jeered. God did not agree. He believed that Job would never curse Him no matter how much Satan mistreated him.

What terrible things happened to Job?

Job's children and servants were killed, and all his animals died. The poor man broke out in terrible sores and sat in a pile of ashes. Job complained, "What did I ever do to deserve this?" But Job accepted his losses and did not curse God. In return, God restored all of Job's wealth and gave him 10 more children.

13

The Ultimate Sacrifice

WHO WAS ABRAHAM?

The father of the Hebrew nation. While other people worshipped many gods and made statues of them, Abraham worshipped only the one God. One day, God appeared to Abraham and said, "Take your family to a new country, and I will make you a great nation." Abraham traveled to Canaan, along with his wife, Sarah, and his brother's son, Lot. Abraham's descendants became known as the Hebrews because they were originally from Hebron.

WHEN DID SARAH GIVE BIRTH TO ISAAC?

When she was 90 years old. Sarah had never been able to have children, which made her very sad. When God told her that she would soon give birth, Sarah couldn't help but laugh. A year later, however, she had a son. She named him Isaac, which means "laughter."

HOW DID GOD TEST ABRAHAM'S LOVE?

God wanted to know if Abraham loved his son, Isaac, more than he loved God. He told Abraham to sacrifice the boy. Sadly, Abraham built an altar and put wood on it. Just as Abraham held a knife above the boy, ready to strike, God stopped him. He saw that Abraham's faith was real.

Lot's Troubles

Where did Lot settle?

Abraham and his nephew Lot became prosperous in Canaan. They owned huge flocks of sheep and herds of cattle which, before long, were crowding the land. So Lot moved to Sodom, on the plains of the Jordan River.

Why was God unhappy with Sodom and Gomorrah?

Both cities were very wicked, so God decided to destroy them. When He told Abraham his plan, the old man begged God to spare Lot. God agreed, and sent two angels to Sodom to warn Lot and his family to leave. "Hurry!" the angels said, "and don't look back."

What happened to Lot's wife?

Lot's family fled from Sodom just before God destroyed the city with a fiery rain of burning tar. As the family ran down the road, Lot's wife turned for one last look—and was turned into a pillar of salt! Today, Sodom lies beneath the Dead Sea. An odd column of salt known as Lot's Wife stands on its rocky shore.

The Lost Birthright

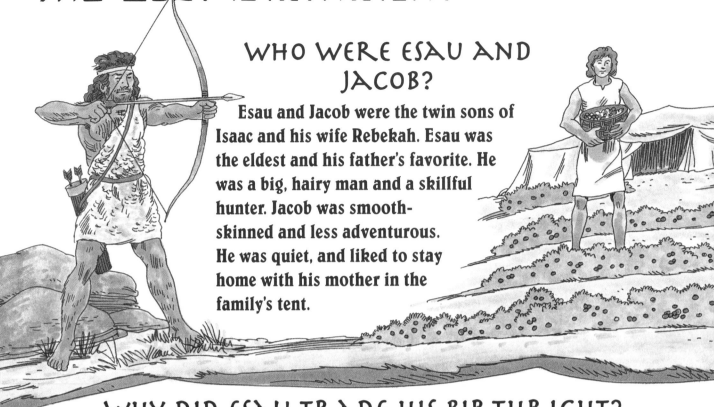

WHO WERE ESAU AND JACOB?

Esau and Jacob were the twin sons of Isaac and his wife Rebekah. Esau was the eldest and his father's favorite. He was a big, hairy man and a skillful hunter. Jacob was smooth-skinned and less adventurous. He was quiet, and liked to stay home with his mother in the family's tent.

WHY DID ESAU TRADE HIS BIRTHRIGHT?

One day, Esau came home from hunting, empty-handed and terribly hungry. Jacob was cooking a lentil stew; Esau asked for a bowl. "I'll trade it for your birthright," Jacob said. This meant that Jacob rather than Esau would inherit Isaac's land, goods, and animals. The famished Esau agreed to the deal but did not intend to honor it.

HOW WAS ISAAC TRICKED?

Isaac was blind, so he was easily tricked into giving Esau's birthright to Jacob. As Isaac lay dying, he asked Esau to cook a roasted meat dish he loved, and then he would bless him. While Esau was out hunting, Rebekah roasted a goat and served the meat to Jacob. She wrapped goatskins around Jacob's arms and chest so that he would seem hairy. Then Jacob took the meat to his father. When Isaac felt the goatskin, he believed that he was blessing Esau.

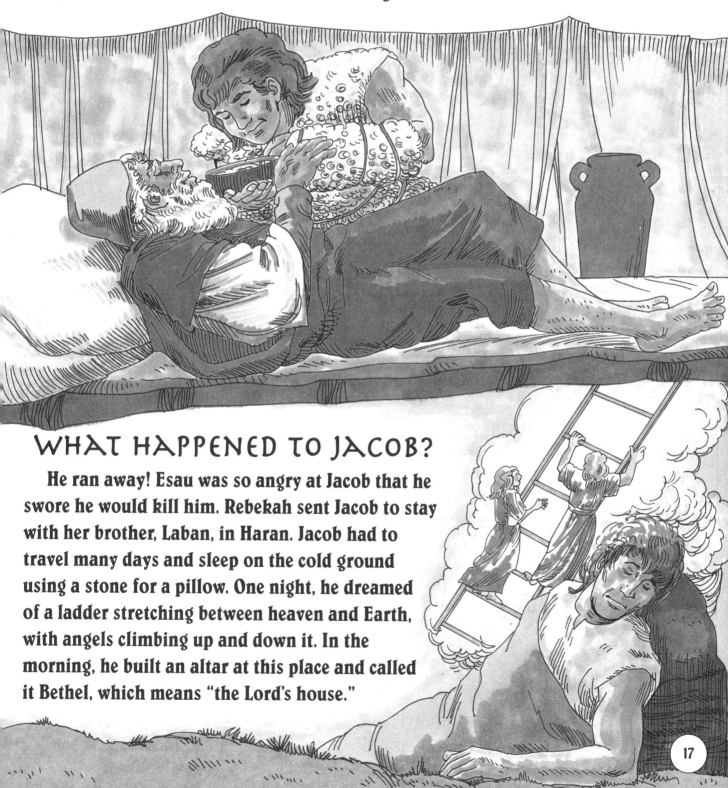

WHAT HAPPENED TO JACOB?

He ran away! Esau was so angry at Jacob that he swore he would kill him. Rebekah sent Jacob to stay with her brother, Laban, in Haran. Jacob had to travel many days and sleep on the cold ground using a stone for a pillow. One night, he dreamed of a ladder stretching between heaven and Earth, with angels climbing up and down it. In the morning, he built an altar at this place and called it Bethel, which means "the Lord's house."

Jacob in Haran

How was Jacob tricked by his uncle?

Jacob fell in love with Laban's daughter, Rachel, but Laban said that he must work seven years to marry her. Jacob did, so Laban took his veiled daughter to the wedding—but it was a trick. Laban had substituted Leah, Rachel's older sister. Jacob had to work seven more years before he could marry his true love.

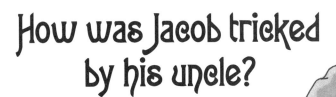

With whom did Jacob wrestle?

An angel. After many years in Haran, God told Jacob to return home. Although Jacob sent gifts to his brother Esau to make peace, he heard that Esau was approaching with a huge army. That night, Jacob prayed for help. He fell asleep and dreamed that he was wrestling with an angel.

What new name did the angel give to Jacob?

Jacob and the angel wrestled all night, but Jacob would not let the angel go. "Give me your blessing," he insisted. The angel struck Jacob's hip instead, which caused Jacob to limp. As dawn broke, the angel finally blessed Jacob, and told him, "Your name now is Israel, which means 'fights with God.'" Jacob looked up and saw Esau and his army approaching.

Did Esau forgive his brother?

When Esau came near, Israel bowed down to the ground seven times and begged his brother for mercy. Esau pulled him up from where he lay and hugged him. All was forgiven, and the brothers became a family once again.

Joseph and the Coat of Many Colors

What was the coat of many colors?

Israel's favorite sons were Joseph and Benjamin, the children he had with Rachel. When Israel gave Joseph a beautiful coat of many colors, the older brothers became jealous. They threw Joseph into a pit. While they were debating whether or not they should kill him, some slave traders happened by, and the brothers sold Joseph into slavery for twenty pieces of silver.

How did Joseph become a powerful governor?

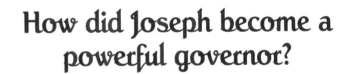

Joseph was bought by Potiphar, an officer in the Egyptian army. Potiphar trusted Joseph like a son. But Potiphar's wife had Joseph thrown into prison. There, Joseph foretold the future by interpreting two prisoners' dreams. News of his ability reached the pharaoh, Egypt's king. Soon Joseph was not only explaining the pharaoh's dreams, but overseeing Egypt as its chief governor.

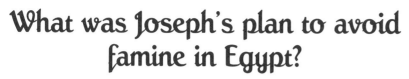

What was Joseph's plan to avoid famine in Egypt?

The pharaoh had a dream foretelling seven years of prosperity and seven years of famine. During the seven years of plenty, Joseph filled Egypt's barns with grain. When the lean years came, Joseph sold the food to the hungry people. Even Joseph's brothers went to Egypt to buy food.

How did the brothers make peace?

When his brothers came to Egypt to buy food, Joseph had them arrested for spying. "You can leave," he told them, "if your youngest brother comes to Egypt." After Benjamin arrived, Joseph sent them all home with sacks of food and money, and then had them re-arrested for stealing. Joseph revealed himself as their long-lost brother, and the older brothers begged his forgiveness. Joseph sent for Israel, his father, and the family lived the rest of its days together in Egypt.

What happened to the 12 brothers?

When Israel was on his deathbed in Egypt, he blessed his 12 sons. "You will father the 12 tribes of Israel," he told them. Later, God divided Canaan among 12 of Israel's sons. The third son, Levi, became the priest of the temple and received no tribal land. However, the other brothers agreed to support him and his descendants.

Moses

Why was the baby Moses put in a basket?

The Israelites prospered and became a powerful people in Egypt. After Joseph's death, a new pharaoh came to power. He ordered the Hebrews to work as the Egyptians' slaves. He also ordered that all Hebrew boy babies be drowned. But one mother made a basket from bulrushes and set her little boy, later to be called Moses, afloat on the river.

Who rescued Moses?

The pharaoh's daughter. She was bathing in the river when she found a baby boy floating in his basket. She decided to raise him as her own son and she named him Moses, which means "pulled from the water." Moses grew up in the palace of the pharaoh.

DON'T CRY!

HE'S CUTE!

How did God speak to Moses?

When Moses was a grown man, he tended sheep in the desert. One day, an angel appeared in a burning bush and told him to go see the pharaoh and demand the Hebrews' freedom.

WOW!

What were the 10 plagues of Egypt?

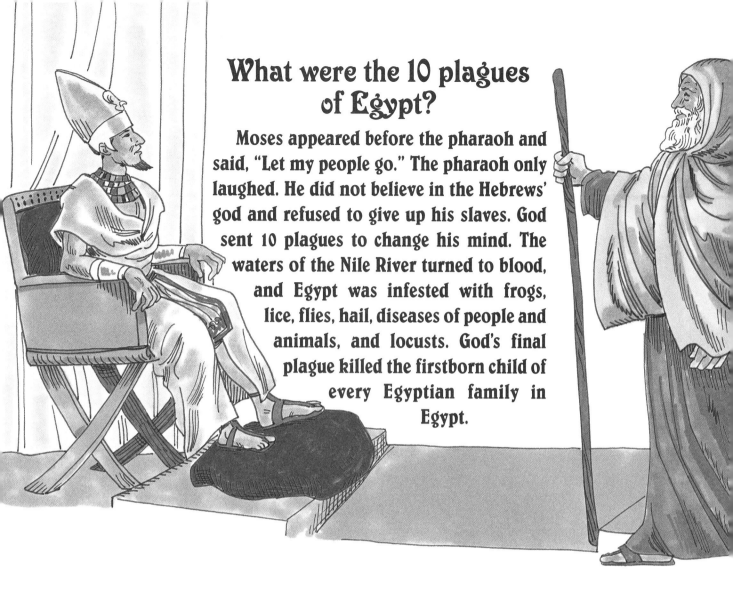

Moses appeared before the pharaoh and said, "Let my people go." The pharaoh only laughed. He did not believe in the Hebrews' god and refused to give up his slaves. God sent 10 plagues to change his mind. The waters of the Nile River turned to blood, and Egypt was infested with frogs, lice, flies, hail, diseases of people and animals, and locusts. God's final plague killed the firstborn child of every Egyptian family in Egypt.

How did the Hebrews save their firstborn sons?

God told Moses, "Tonight I will kill many people, but I will spare everyone who marks their door with lambs' blood." All the Hebrews marked their doors, and their children were spared. The pharaoh's own son, however, died. The frightened pharaoh quickly agreed to give the Hebrews their freedom. The Jewish holiday of Passover celebrates the Hebrews' passing out of Egypt.

THE PARTING OF THE RED SEA

Why did Moses part the Red Sea?

No sooner had the Hebrews left Egypt than the pharaoh changed his mind and ordered his army to recapture them. The army trapped them on the banks of the Red Sea. Moses raised his staff over the water and the sea divided, leaving a path on which the Hebrews could walk to the far shore. When the army tried to follow, the walls of water collapsed and drowned them.

The Ten Commandments

How did Moses receive the Ten Commandments?

Months after fleeing from Egypt, Moses and his people arrived at a mountain called Sinai. Moses climbed to the mountaintop, where he spoke with God. God gave Moses two stone tablets with the Ten Commandments written on them. These were rules for living a good life.

What did the tablets say?

The Commandments were written by God with His own finger. They told the Israelites to worship no other God, to keep the sabbath, and to respect their parents. The Israelites were forbidden to mock God's name, tell lies, kill, steal, be unfaithful to their marriage partners, or to desire anything that belonged to their neighbors. God told Moses that if the Israelites kept His commandments, they would become a holy nation.

What was the Land of Milk and Honey?

Canaan, the land that God had promised to Abraham and his descendants. Moses sent some men to explore Canaan. They returned with a cluster of grapes so large that it took two men to carry it!

Moses never set foot in this Promised Land. He did catch a glimpse of it—he saw Canaan from Mount Nebo before he died at the age of 120. Joshua, Moses' second-in-command, led the Israelites into that new country.

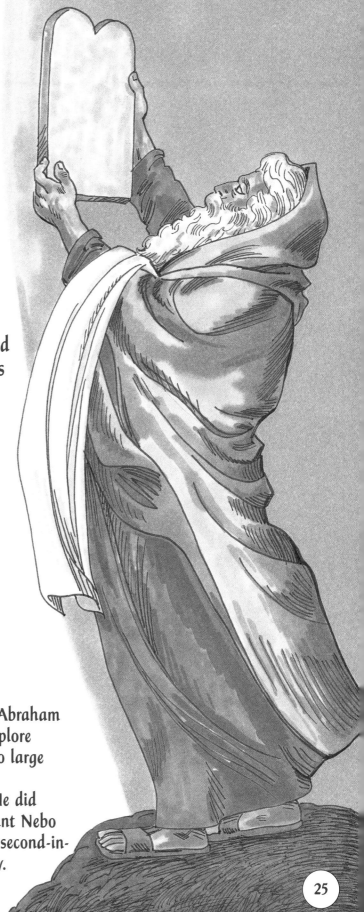

The Ark of the Lord

WHAT WAS THE TABERNACLE?

While in the desert, the Israelites worshipped God in a special tent called the Tabernacle. It had an inner room that contained the Ark of the Covenant. God told Moses exactly how to make the Ark.

WHAT WAS THE ARK OF THE COVENANT?

A wooden chest lined with gold. In the middle of the lid was "the mercy seat," where God sat when He wanted to speak with human beings. Inside were the two tablets of the Ten Commandments.

HOW WAS THE ARK CARRIED?

With poles that were made from acacia wood, and then plated with gold. They were slipped into gold rings on each side of the Ark. God said that the poles should always stay in the rings.

WHEN DID THE ISRAELITES LOSE THE ARK OF THE COVENANT?

The Israelites were fighting a terrible battle against the Philistines. They had already lost 4,000 men when their priests decided to take the Ark to the battleground in hopes that it would inspire the soldiers to rally. The Philistines still triumphed. They stole the Ark and stored it in the temple of their god, Dagon.

HOW WAS THE ARK RECOVERED BY THE ISRAELITES?

The morning after the Ark was placed in the temple of Dagon, the Philistines found their god's statue broken on the floor. Then they developed horrible tumors, and their land was overrun with rats. After seven months, the Philistines had had enough. They decided to send the Ark back to the Israelites. They hitched it to two cows and, without anyone driving the cart, the Ark made its way to the Israelite village of Beth-shemesh.

WHAT HAPPENED TO THE ARK?

The villagers of Beth-shemesh were so excited to see the Ark that a group of them dared to look inside it. They were killed instantly! The villagers, frightened by their loss, did not want to keep the Ark. They sent it to the city of Kiriath-jearim, where it remained until King David took it to Jerusalem. Today, no one knows where the Ark is, or if it still exists.

THE WALLS OF JERICHO

WHY DID JOSHUA ATTACK JERICHO?

God chose Joshua to lead the Israelites into Canaan, the Promised Land. Before they could settle there, however, they had to conquer many strong-walled cities, including Jericho.

THEY'LL NEVER GET US!

WHY DID JOSHUA SEND SPIES TO JERICHO?

The spies were supposed to find out how well Jericho was defended against attack, but they were discovered by soldiers. Luckily, a woman named Rahab hid the men among bushels of flax on her roof. Her house was built into the city wall. When night fell, she lowered the spies by a rope into the desert and they made their way back to camp.

HIDE HERE.

HOW DID JOSHUA CAPTURE JERICHO?

God told Joshua to surround Jericho with his army. Once a day for six days, the army, led by seven priests, walked around the city carrying the Ark of the Covenant and blowing loud blasts on trumpets made from rams' horns. On the seventh day, the army circled the city seven times, and when the priests blew their trumpets, the walls of Jericho collapsed!

THESE GUYS REALLY ROCK!

Woman Warrior

Who were the Hebrew judges?

The Hebrews were governed not by a single leader, but by a series of judges. These religious men and women settled quarrels and matters of law and led the people into battle.

What woman was both a judge and a military leader?

Deborah. When the Israelites were threatened by a powerful enemy named Sisera, Deborah told Barak, leader of the Israelite army, to attack. Knowing that Sisera's army had 900 chariots of iron, Barak thought this was a foolish idea. He challenged Deborah, "If you will go with me, I will go, but if you will not go, neither will I." So Deborah went with him. Together, they led 10,000 men into battle—and to victory.

What happened to Sisera?

After Sisera's army was defeated, he tried to hide in the tent of a woman named Jael. Jael dressed his wounds, but when the exhausted general fell asleep, she drove a tent peg into his temple, killing him. Later, Deborah and Barak sang a song praising Jael as "most blessed of tent-dwelling women."

The Great Gideon

Who was Gideon?

One of the Hebrew judges. He led his people against an attack launched by the Midianites in Canaan.

Who were the Midianites?

A desert tribe who conquered the Israelites. At harvest time, they destroyed many of the Israelites' crops.

Where was Gideon when God told him to lead the Hebrew army?

Gideon was threshing wheat when he noticed an angel sitting under a tree. "You are a brave man," the angel told him. "Go use this strength of yours to free Israel from the power of the Midianites." Gideon was frightened. He offered the angel some food, but the angel touched the dish with his staff and fire sprang up and burned it. This convinced Gideon that he should do as the angel asked.

How did Gideon anger the townspeople?

He tore down his father's altar to their god, Baal.

What did God tell Gideon to do with his army of 32,000 men?

Send most of them home. Gideon told his troops that anyone afraid to fight could leave; 22,000 ran home. The remaining 10,000 men were sent to drink from a spring. Three hundred filled their cupped hands with water and drank. The rest got down on their knees and lapped the water like a dog. God told Gideon to keep those who drank from their hands and dismiss the rest.

What weapons did Gideon's army use to defeat the Midianites?

Gideon divided his 300 men into three companies and gave each soldier a trumpet and an empty jar with a torch inside it. At the signal, the Hebrews rushed upon the Midianite army from all sides, blowing their trumpets, smashing their jars, and waving the torches. The Midianites fled in a panic.

DRINK UP!

?

The Strongest Man in the World

What was the secret of Samson's amazing strength?

Before Samson was born, an angel told his parents that they would have a son who would do God's work. As a sign of his devotion to God, he should never cut his hair. In return, God would give him incredible strength. When Samson became a man, his hair was long and shaggy and his strength was extraordinary. He even killed a lion with his bare hands!

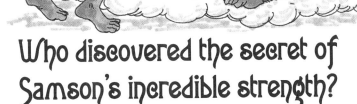

Who discovered the secret of Samson's incredible strength?

Delilah, a beautiful Philistine woman. She badgered Samson until he revealed that if his hair were cut, he would lose his strength. Delilah betrayed his secret to the Philistines, who seized Samson, cut his hair, poked out his eyes, and threw him into prison.

How did Samson die?

The leader of the Philistines threw a great feast and tied Samson to the pillars of his house so that all the guests could mock him. But Samson's hair had begun to grow back and he prayed that his strength would return. Samson pushed down the pillars of the house, causing the roof to cave in on 3,000 Philistines—and himself.

I'M OUT OF HERE!

The Story of Ruth

Who was Ruth?
Why did she go to Judah?

Ruth was the great-grandmother of King David and a distant ancestor of Jesus. She was from Moab, a country near Judah. She married a man who had moved to Moab from Judah with his parents and brother. After the men of the family all died, Ruth's mother-in-law, Naomi, decided to return to Judah. Naomi told Ruth that she should go back to her own family, but Ruth said, "Where you go, I will go," and she went with Naomi to a country that was not her own.

Who was Boaz, and what was Ruth doing when she met him?

Boaz was a wealthy landowner and a distant relative of Naomi. When Naomi and Ruth returned to Judah, they were very poor. To keep them from starving, Ruth followed the people harvesting the barley fields that belonged to Boaz. She picked up whatever grains they dropped. Boaz noticed her working there and took pity on her. He gave her food and sent his greetings to Naomi.

How did Ruth happen to marry Boaz?

She went to the place where Boaz was sleeping and lay down at his feet. When he awoke and found her there, he was moved by her devotion. The next day, he asked her to marry him. Naomi came to live with them, and God soon blessed the couple with a baby boy.

The Last Judge

WHY WAS SAMUEL GIVEN TO THE PRIEST ELI?

Samuel was the son of Hannah. Before Samuel was born, Hannah had prayed for a child. She promised God that if He gave her one, she would give the child to the Lord for his whole life. Hannah gave birth to Samuel soon afterward and, keeping her promise, took him to the temple to live with Eli and serve him.

WHO CALLED SAMUEL THREE TIMES IN ONE NIGHT?

God did. Each time God called him, Samuel ran into Eli's room calling out, "Here I am!" Eli, finally realizing that it was God calling, told the child to go back to bed, saying, "If the voice calls again, say 'Speak, Lord.'" When Samuel heard the voice again, he said "Speak, Lord," and God spoke to him. Samuel became one of the best judges the Hebrews ever had.

The First King

Why did the Hebrews ask Samuel to choose a king for them?

Samuel's sons took bribes and delivered bad judgments. The people decided that they would be better off ruled by a king than by such wicked judges. God guided Samuel to Saul.

Was Saul a good king?

Saul ruled the Israelites for many years. He was victorious in many battles against the Philistines. However, he did not always obey God's commands, so God became displeased with him. Samuel abandoned Saul and refused to help him.

Who was Saul's successor?

God sent Samuel to a man named Jesse who had many sons. When the eighth son came in from tending his sheep, God whispered in Samuel's ear, "This is the one." Samuel blessed this boy, whose name was David, and told him that he would one day be king.

DAVID AND GOLIATH

Who was Goliath?

A Philistine who was about 6 1/2 feet tall. One day, when David was taking food to his brothers, who were in Saul's army, he heard Goliath issue a challenge. "Choose your man to meet me. If he can kill me in a fair fight, we will become your slaves; but if I kill him, you shall be our slaves and serve us." No man among the Israelites wanted to fight this giant—not even Saul.

Who fought Goliath?

David bravely volunteered. As Goliath was laughing at his puny opponent, David took a stone, placed it in his slingshot, and fired. The stone sank into Goliath's forehead, knocking him flat on his face. David ran to the fallen man, took Goliath's own sword, and cut off his head.

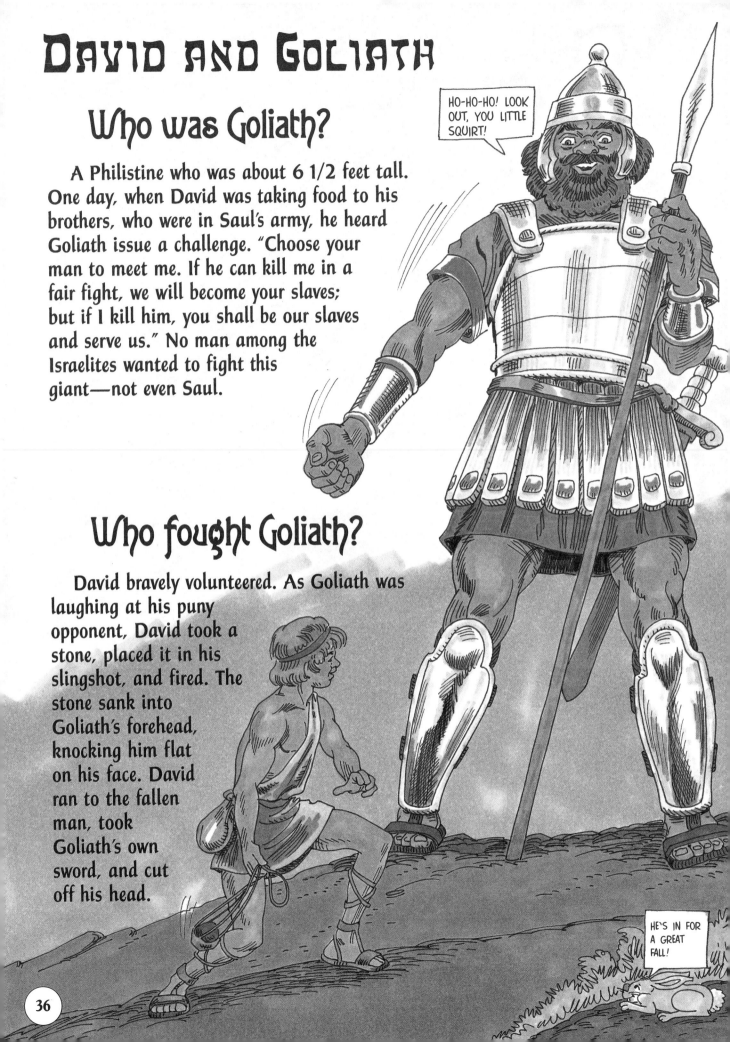

HO-HO-HO! LOOK OUT, YOU LITTLE SQUIRT!

HE'S IN FOR A GREAT FALL!

What happened after David's victory?

King Saul invited David to live with him at the palace. Saul grew to love David like a son. Saul was tormented by bad dreams, because he knew that God was unhappy with him. David, a fine musician, would play the harp to soothe him. When David became a famous soldier, however, Saul became jealous. He worried that the Hebrew people would try to make David king. He even tried to kill David.

When David became king after Saul's death, where did he build his capital city?

Atop a mountain. He called it Jerusalem, which means "City of Peace." Today, it is the capital city of Israel and is often called "The City of David." David decided to bring the Ark of the Covenant to Jerusalem and vowed not to sleep until the job was done. When the Ark was finally safe within the city walls, David was so happy that he danced in the streets.

Why did God punish David?

David fell in love with a beautiful woman named Bathsheba, who was married to a soldier named Uriah. David slyly arranged to have Uriah killed in battle, and then he married Bathsheba himself. God punished David by having Bathsheba's first son die. David repented for his bad behavior and asked God for forgiveness. The couple's second son, Solomon, survived, and became king after David's death.

A Wise King

How did Solomon become so wise?

God spoke to Solomon in a dream and asked him, "What can I give you?" The young king said, "I ask for wisdom, so that I may govern your people justly and distinguish good from evil." God was so pleased with this request that he granted Solomon's wish and gave him wealth and a long life, too.

How did Solomon settle an argument between two mothers?

Both women claimed a baby as their own. Solomon commanded his servant, "Fetch me a sword. Cut the child in two and give half to one and half to the other."

One woman cried out, "Oh, sir, let her have the baby! Whatever you do, do not kill it!" The other said, "Let neither of us have it; cut it in two."

"Give the living baby to the first woman; do not kill it," said the king. "She is its mother."

How large was Solomon's temple?

Solomon built a beautiful temple in Jerusalem to house the Ark of the Covenant. It was 90 feet long and 30 feet wide—huge for that time—and took seven years and 150,000 laborers to build. The temple's walls were cedar outside and overlaid with gold and jewels inside.

Who was the Queen of Sheba, and why did she visit King Solomon?

Solomon's wealth and wisdom were known all over the world. The Queen of Sheba, who ruled a country in Africa, traveled to Israel in order to test his knowledge. She asked Solomon many difficult questions. After hearing his answers she said, "Your wisdom and your prosperity go far beyond the report which I had heard of them."

Chariots of Fire

WHAT IS A PROPHET?

A spokesperson for God. People went to prophets for guidance. Sometimes, however, prophets told people bad news. On those occasions, the prophets were often in danger of being hurt or killed.

WHAT NEWS DID THE PROPHET ELIJAH DELIVER TO KING AHAB?

Elijah warned Ahab that it would not rain until he gave up worshipping a god called Baal. The king was stubborn, however, so his kingdom went for three years without rain.

HOW DID ELIJAH DEFEAT THE PRIESTS OF BAAL?

Elijah decided to prove that the Hebrew God was more powerful than Baal. He took two bulls and laid them on two altars, and then challenged the 450 priests of Baal to set the offering on fire without using any flint or torches. The priests called on Baal, but nothing happened—the offering did not burn. When Elijah called on God, fire shot out of the sky, burning up not only the offering but also the stone altar! This display convinced Ahab. He praised God and had all the priests of Baal killed. God responded by sending rain.

WHY DID ELIJAH HIDE FROM AHAB?

King Ahab's wife, Jezebel, was furious that all the priests of her religion had been killed. She swore to kill Elijah and convinced Ahab to have him arrested. Elijah escaped and hid in the desert.

WHAT HAPPENED TO ELIJAH?

When Elijah was very old, he chose a young man named Elisha to carry on his work. They traveled to the River Jordan, where a chariot of fire swept to the ground and took Elijah up into heaven. According to Jewish tradition, Elijah will someday return to proclaim the coming of the Messiah, the Son of God.

The Beautiful Queen

Who was Esther and what was her secret?

Esther was the beautiful wife of the Persian king, Ahasuerus. She was chosen by him from among all the women in his kingdom. She did not tell him that she was Hebrew, however, because Hebrews were often mistreated by the Persians.

Who saved the king's life?

Mordecai, Esther's cousin, discovered a plot to kill the king. He told Esther, and she let the king know in time to defeat the assassin's plans.

Who was Haman? What did Mordecai do that so angered him?

Haman was an evil officer of the king. When Haman passed through a room, everyone had to bow down to him. Mordecai refused to bow down before anyone but God. This made Haman very angry. He ordered that a gallows be erected to hang Mordecai.

How did Queen Esther save her people by breaking the law?

At Haman's urging, the king passed a law condemning to death all the Hebrews living in his kingdom. To change the king's mind, Esther went to his throne room without being sent for—an act punishable by death—to beg the king to attend a private dinner. The king agreed to come. During the meal, Esther revealed that she was a Hebrew and asked him to spare her life and the lives of her people. The king, angry at Haman, ordered that the law be changed.

How was Mordecai rewarded and Haman punished?

The king asked Haman how he would reward a man who had done the king a great favor. Haman suggested that the man be honored before all the people.

"Do this for Mordecai," said the king. "He saved my life."

Haman was furious, but did as he was commanded. After Haman's wickedness was revealed, the king decreed that Haman would hang on the gallows that had been prepared for Mordecai.

DANIEL IN THE DEN OF LIONS

Who was Nebuchadnezzar?

Nebuchadnezzar was a Babylonian king who conquered Jerusalem and all of Mesopotamia. He took the treasures from Solomon's temple and placed them in Babylon, his capital city.

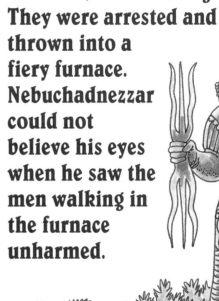

Who was Daniel?

Daniel was a young Hebrew who was taken prisoner when the Babylonians captured Jerusalem. Nebuchadnezzar's servant chose the finest prisoners to go to the palace for training as officers of the court. Daniel and three of his friends were chosen.

What amazing thing happened to Daniel's three friends?

Nebuchadnezzar commanded everyone to bow down before a huge golden statue. Shadrach, Meshach, and Abednego refused. They were arrested and thrown into a fiery furnace. Nebuchadnezzar could not believe his eyes when he saw the men walking in the furnace unharmed.

Who read the writing on the palace wall, and what did it say?

During a banquet, Belshazzar—Nebuchadnezzar's son, who had become king—drank from the golden goblets taken from Solomon's temple. Suddenly, some words appeared on the palace wall. "What are these words?" the frightened king asked.

Only Daniel could interpret them. "Mene mene tekel upharsin," he said, "means that you will soon lose your kingdom—and your life!" That very night, Darius the Mede conquered Babylon and killed Belshazzar.

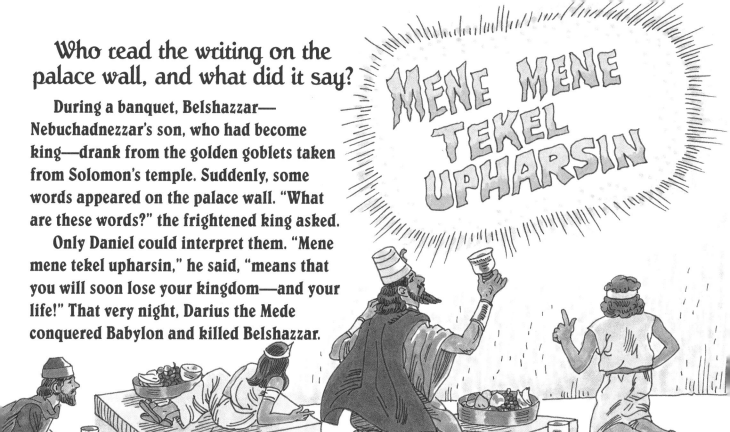

MENE MENE TEKEL UPHARSIN

Why did Darius throw Daniel into a den of lions?

Darius had heard of Daniel's wisdom, so he made him one of the rulers of Babylon. Some of Darius's men became jealous. They convinced the king to pass a law forbidding people to worship anyone but himself. When Daniel continued to pray to God, the jealous men forced Darius to throw Daniel into a den of lions to be torn to pieces. The next morning, Darius shouted, "Daniel, are you alive?"

Daniel answered, "Yes! God has shut the mouths of the lions."

Darius was so amazed, he decreed that everyone in Babylon must worship the Hebrew god.

A Brand-new Wall

When did the Hebrews return to Jerusalem from Babylon?

King Darius was succeeded by Cyrus, who allowed Solomon's temple to be rebuilt and all of its treasures returned. Nehemiah, the king's cupbearer, rebuilt the ruined walls of the city.

What was Nehemiah's plan to rebuild Jerusalem's walls?

Nehemiah knew that Jerusalem would be easy to attack as long as its walls were in ruins, and that the Hebrews' many enemies would not want them rebuilt. He met secretly with some soldiers and divided them into groups of workers and guards. He gave every guard a trumpet and said to the people: "Wherever the trumpet sounds, rally to us there, and God will fight for us."

How many days did it take to rebuild the walls?

Only 52! During all that time, not one of the workers changed his clothes, and not one of the guards laid down his weapon.

While Nehemiah was busy with the walls, who rebuilt the temple?

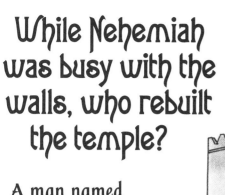

A man named Zerubbabel. Following Solomon's original plan, he worked for four years to complete what was known as the Second Temple. Later, King Herod built a new one, the Third Temple, which eventually was destroyed by the Roman army.

Are any of the temple's walls still standing?

One wall, the Western or Wailing Wall, still stands. It is about 160 feet long and 50 feet high. Today it forms part of the Dome of the Rock, a Muslim temple.

Jonah and the Whale

WHAT MESSAGE DID GOD ASK JONAH TO DELIVER?

God told Jonah, "Go to the great city of Nineveh and denounce it for its wickedness." Jonah was afraid to do this, so he got on a ship sailing in the opposite direction.

WHY DID THE SAILORS THROW JONAH OVERBOARD?

No sooner had the ship set sail than a huge storm broke. When the sailors discovered that Jonah was the cause of the storm, they reluctantly threw him overboard. At that moment, the storm subsided and a great whale came along and swallowed Jonah.

GULP!

HOW LONG WAS JONAH IN THE BELLY OF THE WHALE?

He lay there for three days and nights before finally praying for forgiveness. God then commanded the whale to spit Jonah onto the shore. Jonah then traveled to Nineveh where the people believed his message. They began to fast and pray, begging God to show them mercy. Nineveh was spared.

WHY DID JONAH BECOME ANGRY WITH GOD?

Jonah knew that God is merciful and would spare the city if people repented. Jonah was angry and embarrassed that he had gone through so much trouble for nothing.

WHAT MIRACLE DID GOD PERFORM TO CHANGE JONAH'S MIND?

When Jonah sat down on a hill, God caused a plant to grow up over Jonah's head to shade him. Then he sent a worm to kill the plant. Without shade, the sun beat down so hard that Jonah became very uncomfortable and very angry. But God said, "You worry too much about your comfort. The 120,000 people of Nineveh are much more worthy of your attention."

YUM!

Old Testament Miracles

Who was Aaron and what happened to his staff?

Aaron was Moses' brother and the chief priest of the Tabernacle. Some of the Israelites told Moses that they did not want Aaron to rule over them. "Give me your staffs," Moses told the other would-be leaders. He put these in the Tabernacle. The next day, Aaron's staff had sprouted flowers and almonds. This convinced the doubters that Aaron was God's choice as chief priest.

MOVE, MOVE, MOVE!

Why did Balaam's donkey refuse to go forward?

God commanded Balaam, a prophet, to stay home, but Balaam saddled his donkey and set out. This made God angry. He sent an angel to stand in the middle of the road with a sword in his hand. The donkey, seeing the angel, suddenly veered into a wall. Balaam, who could not see the angel, began hitting the donkey. "What have I done to you, that you have struck me these three times?" the beast asked him. Balaam, amazed to hear it speak, fell on his knees and begged God's forgiveness.

What happened when the Israelites carried the Ark of the Covenant into the Jordan River?

The waters parted and they were able to cross the riverbed into Canaan. This occurred after Moses' death, when Joshua led the Israelites into the Promised Land.

How did God punish the children who laughed at the prophet Elisha?

When Elisha was an old man, he was taunted by some young boys.

"Get along with you, bald head, get along," they jeered. Elisha turned around and cursed them in the name of God. Suddenly, two female bears came out of the woods and ate the boys.

What did the prophet Isaiah do to the sun?

He made it go backward, to demonstrate God's power to Hezekiah, a king of Judah.

When did the sun stand still?

Joshua and the Israelites were fighting their enemies in Canaan. Joshua cried out, "Stand still, O sun; stand, moon." God stopped the sun from setting and the moon from rising until the armies of Israel were completely victorious.

WHAT IS THE NEW TESTAMENT?

The New Testament is made up of 27 books. They are about Jesus and early Christianity. The events described in these books took place about 400 years after the events in the last book of the Old Testament. The first four New Testament books are biographies of Jesus. The fifth book, called the Acts of the Apostles, describes how Jesus' followers preached the good news about Jesus. The next 21 books are letters, called epistles. The first 14 epistles are named for the people to whom they are addressed. The remaining seven are named for their authors. The final book, Revelation, foretells the end of the world.

WHAT IS THE GOSPEL?

The word *gospel* means "good news." It refers to the four books in the New Testament that tell about the life, death, and resurrection (return to life) of Jesus. The books, which were written by four different men—Matthew, Mark, Luke, and John—share many of the same stories.

WHO WAS THE MESSIAH?

In the Old Testament, prophets said that God would send a Messiah, or savior, who would free the Jewish people from their oppressors and be their king. According to Jesus' followers, who were the authors of the New Testament, Jesus was the Messiah. They believed that His death made it possible for people to enter the kingdom of God. According to the Book of Revelation, Jesus will return to Earth again and reign as king in Jerusalem.

WHEN AND WHERE DID JESUS LIVE?

Jesus lived from about 4 B.C. to 30 A.D. in the land of Israel. During that time, this area was part of the Roman Empire.

Two Babies

Who was Zechariah?

An elderly priest who lived in Judea with his wife, Elizabeth. They were sad because they had no children.

Who told Zechariah that his wife would have a son?

An angel. Zechariah was burning incense in the temple when the angel Gabriel appeared, saying, "Your wife will bear a son. You shall name him John, and he will be great in the eyes of the Lord."

Why couldn't Zechariah talk for nine months?

Zechariah protested that Elizabeth was too old to have a child. The angel said, "Because you have not believed me, you will lose your power of speech and remain silent until the day when these things happen to you." Zechariah left the temple mute and was unable to speak for the next nine months.

When did he speak again?

When Elizabeth gave birth to a son, all of the friends and relatives assumed that the boy would be named after his father. To their astonishment, his mother said, "No! He is to be called John." When Zechariah wrote the name John on a tablet, his lips and tongue were freed. Their son grew up to be John the Baptist, a famous prophet.

Who else did the angel Gabriel speak to?

Elizabeth's young cousin, Mary. She was at her home in Nazareth when Gabriel appeared. He told Mary that she, too, would have a baby. This child was born after Mary married Joseph, a carpenter. Her son was Jesus Christ, the Messiah or "promised one."

The Baby Jesus

Why did Mary and Joseph go to Bethlehem?

The Emperor Augustus wanted to know how many people lived in the Roman Empire. He passed a law stating that all people must return to the city where they were born to be counted. So Joseph left Nazareth for Bethlehem, where he had been born.

Where was Jesus born?

In a stable. Mary was due to have her baby when the couple arrived in Bethlehem. They tried to find an inn where they could stay, but the city was crowded with visitors. They took shelter in a stable, where Mary delivered her son. His cradle was a manger, a feeding trough for the animals.

Who did an angel tell of Jesus' birth?

Some shepherds looking after their flocks. The angel appeared and told them that "a Savior" was born on this day. After the angel went away, the shepherds went to find the baby.

Who gave Jesus gifts of rare spices and perfumes and how did they find him?

Three wise men from the East. They had seen a brilliant star in the night sky, and they traveled to Jerusalem, following the star. The star hovered over the place where the baby Jesus lay.

Who was frightened by Jesus' birth?

Herod, the king of Israel. The three wise men told him that the "king of the Jews" had just been born, and Herod was afraid that this child would someday challenge his rule. Since Herod did not know where Jesus was, he decreed that *all* the male babies in Bethlehem must be killed. This tragedy became known as the Slaughter, or Massacre, of the Innocents.

Why did Joseph take his family to Egypt?

An angel appeared to Joseph and told him to flee into Egypt in order to save Jesus' life. The family did not return to Israel until Herod died. Then they went back to Nazareth, where Mary and Joseph had lived before.

Jesus Gets Lost

Why did Mary, Joseph, and Jesus go from Nazareth to Jerusalem?

To celebrate the Passover. This was a popular thing to do, so the city was crowded with visitors.

GALILEE

Nazareth

Sea of Galilee

River Jordan

SAMARIA

Dead Sea

Jerusalem

JUDEA

HOW DO I GET THERE?

How long was Jesus lost in Jerusalem?

As they were traveling home, Jesus' parents realized that their 12-year-old son was no longer with them. Mary and Joseph returned to Jerusalem, where they spent three days searching for Jesus.

I HAVE NOT SEEN THE BOY.

WHERE CAN HE BE?

WE'VE LOOKED FOR THREE DAYS!

JESUS, WHERE ARE YOU?

Where was he found?

His anxious parents finally found Jesus in the temple built by Herod the Great. He was sitting in the middle of a group of learned men, asking—and answering—questions about God and religious law.

What did Jesus say to his parents when they found him?

"What made you search? Did you not know that I was supposed to be in my Father's house?" (In other words, "Where else would I be but in the temple?")

Where else did Jesus travel besides Jerusalem?

In his lifetime, Jesus visited only the three regions of Palestine: Galilee (where he grew up), Judea, and Samaria. He traveled fewer than 100 miles from home in all his life.

The Voice in the Wilderness

WHO WAS "THE VOICE IN THE WILDERNESS"?

Many years before Jesus' birth, the prophet Isaiah predicted: "A voice crying aloud in the wilderness will say, 'Prepare a way for the Lord; clear a straight path for him.'" That voice belonged to John the Baptist. He lived in the desert, wearing clothes made from camel hair, and eating wild honey and locusts. Crowds of people went to hear him preach and to be baptized by him.

WHAT IS BAPTISM? WHY DID JOHN BAPTIZE PEOPLE?

To baptize means "to make pure and clean." John baptized people in the River Jordan to cleanse them of their sins.

WHY DID JESUS WANT TO BE BAPTIZED?

Jesus did not need to be baptized, because he was sinless, but he wanted to set an example for others. He went to see John, who dipped him in the River Jordan. After Jesus was baptized, a dove descended from heaven and rested on Him. A voice from heaven said, "This is my beloved son, in whom I am well pleased."

WHO THREW JOHN INTO PRISON?

Herod Antipas, the ruler of Galilee, who was the son of Herod the Great. John had criticized him for marrying his brother's wife, which was against Jewish law.

WHO WAS SALOME?

Herod's stepdaughter, the daughter of his brother's wife. A gifted dancer, she performed for Herod at his birthday party. He asked her what she would like as a reward for her performance, and she requested—and received—the head of John the Baptist on a platter.

The Temptations of Jesus

Why did Jesus go into the wilderness?

The Holy Spirit led Him there to fast (not eat or drink) and pray for 40 days. While He was in the wilderness, He was tested by the devil three times.

What were the tests and how did Jesus respond?

First, Satan said, "If you are the Son of God, tell these stones to become bread."

Jesus replied, "Man does not live by bread alone; he lives on every word that God utters."

Next, Satan took Jesus to the roof of the temple and said, "If you are the Son of God, throw yourself down."

Jesus answered, "You are not to put the Lord your God to the test."

Finally, Satan offered Jesus all the power and glory and riches of the world if He would only worship evil, but Jesus refused.

Jesus Finds the Apostles

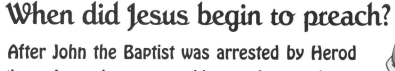

When did Jesus begin to preach?

After John the Baptist was arrested by Herod Antipas, Jesus began preaching to the people. He was about 30 years old at the time. He preached for three years, until his death.

What miracle did Jesus perform at the Sea of Galilee?

Jesus asked Simon, a fisherman, to take him out in his boat, so that he could preach to all the people crowded on the shore. When Jesus finished speaking, he told Simon, "Drop your nets." When Simon did, so many fish filled the nets that the boat nearly sank.

What happened to the fishermen?

After they unloaded their catch, Simon and three other fishermen decided to leave their trade and become "fishers of men." They became disciples, or followers, of Jesus.

Special Friends

Who were Jesus' apostles and what did they do?

Jesus chose 12 of his disciples to be his apostles—people with a special mission. The apostles were Simon (called Peter) and his brother, Andrew; James and John, sons of Zebedee; Philip; Bartholomew; Thomas; Matthew; James, son of Alphaeus; Thaddaeus; Simon the Zealot; and Judas Iscariot. They helped Jesus to teach and preach about God.

Which apostle was called "the rock" and why?

Simon. He was called Peter, which means "the rock." Jesus said of him: "Upon this rock I will build my church." After Jesus' death, Peter worked hard to spread Jesus' teachings and to build his church.

Who was the youngest apostle?

John. Jesus asked John to take care of His mother, Mary, after His death.

What was Matthew's profession before he became an apostle?

He was a tax collector. Collecting taxes from the Jews for their Roman rulers was not a popular job. Jesus was criticized by other Jews for having a tax collector as a friend.

Early Miracles

What did Mary, Jesus' mother, ask her son to do at the wedding feast in Cana?

During the celebration, Mary noticed that there was no more wine. She asked Jesus to do something about this, so Jesus told the servants to fill six jugs with water. When the servants poured from the jugs, wine came out instead of water!

What did nine of the ten lepers forget to do after Jesus cured them?

Thank him. The healed lepers ran away to celebrate their good fortune. Only one returned to praise and thank Jesus.

Who did Jesus heal without ever seeing him?

The servant of a commander in the Roman army. The Roman approached Jesus and begged him to heal his servant. Jesus told the man to go home, where he found his servant cured.

What did Jesus say to the sick woman who sneaked up behind him to touch the hem of his robe?

Jesus felt her touch and turned to her, saying, "Daughter, your faith has saved you. Go in peace, and be well from now on." She was immediately healed.

When Jesus walked on the water, who did he tell to come over to him?

Peter. During a storm, Jesus left the shore and walked across the water to meet his apostles, who were struggling to row their boat. Peter stepped out of the boat and walked over the water toward Jesus, but he soon became afraid and began to sink. Jesus said, "Oh ye of little faith," and lifted Peter back into the boat.

What was the the Transfiguration?

Jesus took some of the apostles to a mountain, where He was changed, or "transfigured." His face shone like the sun and His clothes glowed with light. The apostles saw Moses and Elijah appear and talk with Jesus. Then a voice from the sky said, "This is my beloved Son, in whom I am very pleased. Listen to Him."

THE SERMON ON THE MOUNT

WHAT DID JESUS TELL HIS LISTENERS IN THE SERMON ON THE MOUNT?

He described how people need to behave in order to please God and enter into heaven. One of Jesus' most important messages that day became what is known as "the Golden Rule": "Always treat others as you would like them to treat you."

WHY WAS THIS CALLED THE SERMON ON THE MOUNT?

So many people had come to hear Jesus speak, He had to walk up the side of a hill so they all could hear and see Him as He preached.

WHAT PRAYER DID HE SAY ON THAT DAY?

The Lord's Prayer. It begins: "Our Father who art in heaven, hallowed be thy name. Thy kingdom come, thy will be done on Earth as it is in heaven."

The Miracle of the Loaves and Fishes

When Jesus preached on the shore of the Sea of Galilee, what did one little boy have that none of the thousands of other listeners had?

Food. The boy had five loaves of bread and two fish to eat. No one else among the crowds who had come to hear Jesus that day had any food with them.

What did Jesus do with the basket of bread and fish?

He miraculously made those five loaves and two fish feed about 5,000 men, plus women and children—and there were 12 baskets of leftovers.

What did Jesus tell the people who wanted him to feed them the next day?

"I am the Bread of Life," he said. "Whoever comes to me shall never be hungry, and whoever believes in me shall never be thirsty." Jesus was talking about the hunger and thirst that people have in their hearts rather than in their stomachs.

The Parables

What is a parable?

A story that teaches. Jesus used parables to tell people how to treat one another and how to better love God.

What happened in the parable of the sower?

A farmer was sowing seeds. Some were eaten by birds. Others either fell among rocks and could not take root or were choked by weeds. Only those that fell on good soil bore fruit. The failed seeds, Jesus said, represent people who hear God's word but do not believe or follow it, while the seeds that grow represent the people who do.

Why did the king become angry with the servant who owed him money?

The servant owed the king a large sum of money. The king kindly forgave the debt. Later, however, he heard that the same servant had put in jail a neighbor who owed him a very small sum of money. The king became so angry that he imprisoned the servant who had owed him money until he could pay his debt in full. "Forgive others as God forgives you" is the moral of this parable.

What did the prodigal (wasteful) son do after spending his father's money foolishly?

He took a job caring for pigs, but was given nothing to eat. He decided to return home to beg forgiveness and ask if he could work as one of his father's servants. Instead of punishing him, his father kissed and welcomed him, and organized a big party in his honor. "This is how it is with God," Jesus explained. "When people are truly sorry, He forgives them and welcomes them back."

What is the parable of the Good Samaritan?

A Jewish man traveling from Jerusalem to Jericho was set upon by robbers and left to die on the side of the road. Two religious leaders came along at different times, but moved quickly to the other side of the road without helping him. The next traveler to come along was from Samaria. The Jews and Samaritans hated each other, but the Samaritan traveler not only stopped, he dressed the man's wounds, lifted him to the back of his donkey, and took him to the nearest inn to recover. Jesus told this story to explain that God's command to "love your neighbor" includes loving your enemies.

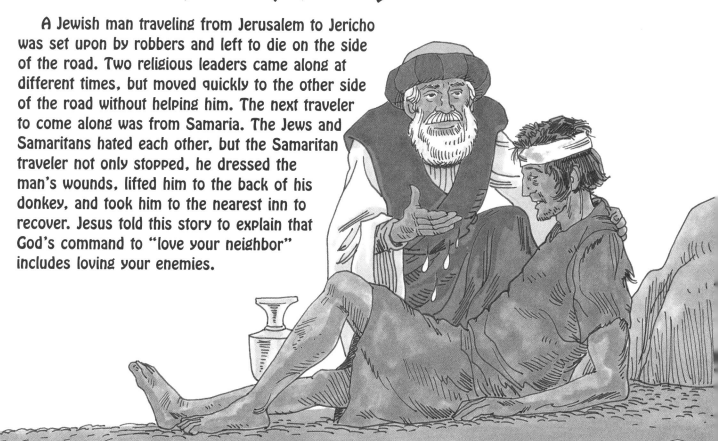

Risen From the Dead!

Who were Mary and Martha?

Mary and Martha were the sisters of Lazarus, one of Jesus' best friends.

How did Jesus help Lazarus?

Lazarus became very sick and died. Jesus arrived after the funeral and walked with the grieving sisters to their brother's tomb. "Roll it away," Jesus said, pointing to the stone that blocked the tomb. They did, and a man emerged from the tomb. It was Lazarus, risen from the dead!

How many other people did Jesus raise from the dead?

Two. Jesus also revived the only son of a widow in the city of Nain and the young daughter of Jarius, a religious leader.

What other prophets and preachers had the power to raise the dead?

The prophets Elisha and Elijah resurrected the sons of widows. The apostle Peter resurrected a woman named Dorcas, who had filled her days with acts of kindness and charity.

THE PHARISEES

WHO WERE THE PHARISEES AND WHAT DID JESUS SAY ABOUT THEM?

They were members of a powerful religious group. They followed Jewish law and tradition very strictly. Jesus believed that the Pharisees were proud and heartless.

WHAT DID THE PHARISEES THINK ABOUT JESUS?

They thought that he did not follow religious laws as strictly as he should. They also disapproved of his preaching to Samaritans, tax collectors, and known sinners—all of whom the Pharisees hated.

WHAT WAS JESUS' RESPONSE TO THIS?

He said, "It is not the healthy who need a doctor, but the sick," meaning that virtuous people needed him less than sinners did.

WHY DID THE PHARISEES FEAR JESUS AND HOW DID THEY PLAN TO LESSEN HIS INFLUENCE?

The Pharisees did not believe that Jesus was the Messiah. They were afraid that His preaching and miracles would convince people that He was the Son of God and that people would then abandon the old religious ways to follow Jesus. They thought if they could get Jesus to break both Jewish and Roman laws, His followers would abandon him and the Romans would punish Him.

WHO DID THE PHARISEES CONVINCE TO BETRAY JESUS?

Judas Iscariot, one of Jesus' own apostles. The Pharisees promised to pay Judas 30 pieces of silver to lead a group of soldiers and police to a quiet place where Jesus could be arrested easily—a place where his crowd of followers could not see what was happening and possibly interfere.

HOW DID THEY TRY TO TRAP JESUS?

One Pharisee asked him, "Are we or are we not permitted to pay taxes to the Roman emperor [Caesar]?" Jesus, who realized this question was a trick, asked to see a coin. "Whose head is on this and whose inscription?" He asked. "Caesar's," was the reply. "Pay Caesar what is due to Caesar," said Jesus, "and pay God what is due to God."

Entrance into Jerusalem

How did the townspeople in Jerusalem honor Jesus' arrival?

They threw their clothes onto the road before Him and cut palm fronds off the trees, spreading them in His path to show their respect. This event is celebrated by Christians each year on Palm Sunday.

HE IS HERE!

WELCOME.

What did Jesus do when He entered the temple in Jerusalem?

He upset the tables of the peddlers and money-changers doing business there. He drove out everyone who was buying and selling, saying, "My house shall be called a house of prayer; but you are making it a robbers' cave."

The Last Supper

What was the Last Supper and what happened during it?

It was the last meal that Jesus and the apostles ate together. It was also their celebration of Passover. During the meal, Jesus told the apostles that one of them would soon betray Him. He gave bread to them, saying "This is my body." Then He took a cup full of wine, and said, "Drink from it. For this is my blood, shed for many for the forgiveness of sins. From this day on, whenever you eat this bread or drink this wine, remember me."

Why did Jesus wash the apostles' feet?

To show them that they must serve one another. This act, which usually was performed by servants, was considered dirty.

77

The Garden at Gethsemane

What did Jesus do after the Last Supper?

He went into the Garden of Gethsemane to pray. He asked God for courage and strength to face the death that He knew awaited Him.

Why was Jesus disappointed with the apostles, and what did He tell them?

They fell asleep while Jesus was praying. He was sorry that they were not awake to prepare for the hard time ahead. He told them that before the night was over, they would all disown Him. Jesus told Peter that he, in particular, would deny knowing Him before the rooster crowed at dawn.

Who betrayed Jesus to the priests and soldiers with a kiss?

Judas Iscariot. Judas kissed Jesus as a sign to the soldiers that he was the man to arrest.

What did Peter do in an attempt to protect Jesus?

He took his sword and cut off the ear of the servant to the high priest. Jesus healed the man's ear saying, "Put up your sword. All who live by the sword die by the sword."

What did Peter do three times before the rooster crowed?

He denied that he knew Jesus. He did this because he was afraid that he, too, would be killed. Once Peter realized that he had done what Jesus had foretold, he sat down and cried.

What happened to Judas after Jesus' death?

He was filled with despair at his betrayal. He threw the silver coins down in the temple, and then hanged himself. The priests used the money to buy a "potter's field," a place to bury people too poor to pay for their own burial.

THE CRUCIFIXION

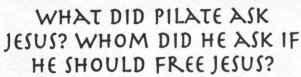

WHAT DID PILATE ASK JESUS? WHOM DID HE ASK IF HE SHOULD FREE JESUS?

He asked, "Are you the king of the Jews?" to which Jesus replied, "My kingdom does not belong to this world." Pilate went back to the priests and said, "I find no case against Him." Then he went before the Jews and said, "You have a custom that I release one prisoner for you at Passover. Would you like me to release the king of the Jews?" The people yelled, "Not Jesus; we want Barabbas!" Pilate took water and washed his hands in full view of the people, saying, "My hands are clean of this man's [Jesus'] blood; see to that yourselves." Then he freed Barabbas, who was a robber, and ordered Jesus to be put to death by crucifixion.

WHAT DID JESUS CARRY THROUGH THE STREETS OF JERUSALEM? WHO HELPED HIM DO THIS?

Jesus was forced to carry a wooden cross—from which He would hang—to Golgotha, a site of executions. At one point, Jesus stumbled and then a man named Simon carried the cross for Him.

WHAT WERE JESUS' LAST WORDS AND WHAT HAPPENED THE MOMENT HE DIED?

First Jesus cried out, "My God, my God, why have You forsaken me?" A short while later, He said, "Father, into your hands I commit my spirit." Then He died. At that moment there was an earthquake, and the curtain that hung in the temple at Jerusalem was torn in two, from top to bottom.

WHAT DID THE SOLDIERS DO AFTER THEY NAILED JESUS TO THE CROSS?

They drew lots to see who would get different items of His clothing. On the cross, over Jesus' head, they placed a sign that read, "This is Jesus, King of the Jews." It was intended to mock Jesus.

The Resurrection

Who arranged for Jesus' burial?

Joseph of Arimathea. He arranged for Jesus to be buried in a tomb cut into the rock of a nearby garden. A huge boulder blocked the tomb's entrance.

Who went to Jesus' tomb to prepare His body for burial?

Mary of Magdala and two other women. They found that the rock that had sealed the tomb had been rolled back and that the body of Jesus was gone. An angel appeared and told the women that Jesus had risen. Then Jesus himself appeared and sent them away to tell the apostles to meet Him in Galilee.

What did the Roman soldiers tell the chief priests?

Soldiers stood guard at the tomb to make sure that Jesus' followers did not steal His body away. They told the chief priests that an angel had rolled back the stone. The priests bribed the soldiers to say that Jesus' disciples had come in the night and stolen the body while they were asleep.

Whom did Mary Magdalene meet in the garden? What did He say to her?

When Mary Magdalene went to the tomb and found it empty, she began to weep. Suddenly, a man she thought was the gardener approached her. "Why are you weeping?" He asked, and immediately she recognized Jesus. When she rushed to embrace Him, He said, "Don't touch me. I have not yet ascended to my Father."

What do Christians call Jesus' return after His death?

The resurrection, which means "the return to life." Easter celebrates Jesus' resurrection.

The Risen Jesus Appears

What happened on the road to Emmaus?

Two of Jesus' followers were walking to a village called Emmaus when a stranger appeared. The three discussed Jesus' death. That evening they ate together and the stranger blessed the bread, broke it and then offered it to the other two men. When this happened, they realized that the stranger was Jesus Himself.

When Jesus first appeared before the apostles, how did they respond?

They thought that He was a ghost and they were terribly frightened. Jesus asked them to touch Him, saying, "No ghost has flesh and bones as you can see that I have."

Which apostle was not present?

Thomas. When Thomas heard the story of Jesus' return, he did not believe it. To convince Thomas later that He really had risen from the dead, Jesus said, "Put your fingers in my wounds." Thomas did so and exclaimed, "My Lord!"

Jesus then said, "Because you have seen me, you have found faith. Happy are they who never saw me and yet have found faith."

The nickname "Doubting Thomas," used for someone who needs convincing, arose from this incident.

The Ascension

HOW LONG DID JESUS STAY ON EARTH AFTER HIS DEATH?

Forty days. During this time, He told the apostles that they should continue to preach. On the fortieth day, Jesus ascended, or rose, into a cloud from a place called Bethany. This was called the Ascension.

AFTER JESUS ASCENDED INTO HEAVEN, WHO APPEARED BEFORE THE APOSTLES?

Two angels. They said, "Why stand there looking up into the sky? This Jesus, who has been taken away from you up to heaven, will come in the same way as you have seen Him go." The apostles returned to Jerusalem with great joy.

THE APOSTLES BEGIN TO PREACH

What happened on Pentecost?

The apostles were together on Pentecost, a harvest festival, when there came a strong wind. Tongues of fire rested on the apostles' heads, and they began to speak in many languages.

How many people were baptized that day?

About 3,000. Jews from all over had come to Jerusalem to celebrate Pentecost. When the foreign visitors heard the apostles preaching in their languages, they stopped to listen. Those who accepted their word were baptized.

Who healed the man who was crippled since birth?

Peter. The man stretched out his hand to beg, but when Peter grasped his hand and pulled him up, his feet and ankles suddenly grew strong and he began to walk.

Why were the apostles arrested?

They were telling people that Jesus had risen from the dead. This was considered blasphemy—a lie about God. The apostles were warned to stop preaching, but they refused. The next time they were arrested, they were imprisoned. An angel released them from prison and told them to go to the temple and preach to the people there. When the Pharisees found the apostles in the temple, they beat them, but the apostles continued to preach.

Who was the first of Jesus' followers to die willingly for his religious beliefs?

Stephen. He was one of seven men the original followers had chosen to help them preach. He performed many miracles. The priests accused him of blasphemy, and he was found guilty and stoned to death. His last words were, "Lord, do not hold this sin against them."

How did Peter die?

The Bible does not mention Peter's death. According to tradition, however, the Roman Emperor Nero ordered that Peter be crucified, upside down, in Rome.

The Road to Damascus

WHO WAS SAUL OF TARSUS?

An educated Jewish man who persecuted (harassed or attacked) any Jew who spoke of Jesus or followed his teachings.

WHERE DID GOD FIRST SPEAK TO SAUL?

Saul was traveling to Damascus to investigate some synagogues rumored to be interested in Jesus' teachings. A bright light shone down from the sky and blinded him. A voice said, "Saul, Saul, why do you persecute me?" Saul was taken to Damascus, where a follower of Jesus laid his hands on him. Something that looked like fish scales fell from Saul's eyes, and he regained his sight. From that day on, he preached that Jesus was the Messiah. (Saul was later known as Paul.)

HOW FAR DID PAUL TRAVEL IN HIS ZEAL TO PREACH?

Paul was the first person to preach in foreign countries. He traveled to Greece, Macedonia, Crete, Sicily, and Rome, as well as all over the Middle East—nearly 1,000 miles. Paul wrote that the salvation Jesus offered was meant for everyone—Gentiles (non-Jews) as well as Jews.

WHY WAS PAUL FORCED TO LEAVE DAMASCUS IN A BASKET?

When Paul became a follower of Jesus, the Jews in Damascus were very suspicious and angry, and they decided to kill him. His friends waited until nightfall, and then lowered him over the city wall in a basket.

WHAT ARE PAUL'S EPISTLES?

The letters that Paul wrote, mostly during a two-year period when he was imprisoned in Rome. These letters, which talk about Jesus' teachings and the new church, became part of the Bible.

Revelations and Prophesies

What is the last book of the Bible?

Revelation, which contains the prophesies of the apostle John. It foretells the end of the world and the coming of the kingdom of God, centered in the new Jerusalem.

What do the seven seals represent?

John wrote that he saw Jesus open a scroll "sealed up with seven seals" that revealed the secrets of the future, including coming disasters in the world. When Jesus broke the first four seals, four horses appeared: a white horse, representing Christ conquering the enemies of God; a red horse, representing war; a black horse, representing famine; and a pale horse, representing death.

What is Armageddon?

John says that it is the last battle that will be fought before the end of the world. It will be a terrible and bloody battle between the forces of good and evil. The forces faithful to God will be victorious, and there will be a new heaven and Earth. The new holy city of Jerusalem will descend from heaven.

What will new Jerusalem look like?

John says that the city will be in the shape of a perfect square, and made "of pure gold, bright as clear glass." The foundations of the city wall will be "adorned with jewels of every kind." There will be no night, and the city will not need light or sun because it will shine with the glory of God.

Index

Leah, 18, 20
Lepers, 66
Levi, 21
Leviticus, the book of, 7
Lord's Prayer, the, 68
Lot, 14-15
Luke, 52

M

Macedonia, 88
Major Prophets, 7
Mark, 52
Martha, 72
Mary (mother of Jesus), 55-59, 65-66
Mary (sister of Lazarus), 72
Mary Magdalene, 82-83
Massacre of the Innocents, 57
Matthew, 52, 64-65
Meshach, 44
Mesopotamia, 44
Messiah, the, 41, 53, 55, 57, 75, 88
Midianites, 30-31
Milk and honey, land of, 25
Minor Prophets, 7
Miracle of the loaves and fishes, 69
Miracles
    in the Old Testament, 50-51, 73
    in the New Testament, 66-67, 69,
        72-73, 75, 86
Moab, 33
Mordecai, 42-43
Moses, 7, 22-26, 50, 67
Mount Nebo, 25
Muslims, 47

N-O

Nain, 73
Naomi, 33
Nazareth, 55-58
Nebuchadnezzar (king of Babylon),
    44-45
Nehemiah, 46
Nero (emperor of Rome), 87
New Jerusalem, 90-91
New Testament, 6
    definition of, 6, 52
    questions concerning, 53-91
Nineveh, 48-49
Noah, 11
Nod, Land of, 10
Numbers, the book of, 7
Old Testament, 6, 52-53
    definition of, 6-7
    questions concerning, 8-51

P

Palestine, 59
Palm Sunday, 76
Parables, the, 70-71
Passover, 23, 58, 77, 80
Paul (Saul of Tarsus), 88-89
Pentecost, the, 86
Persia, 42

Peter (Simon), 63-64, 67, 73, 78-79,
    86-87
Pharaoh (of Exodus), 22-24
Pharisees, the, 74-75, 87
Philip, 64
Philistines, 27, 32, 35-36
Pilate, see PONTIUS PILATE
Plagues of Egypt, 23
Poetical Books, the, 7
Pontius Pilate, 80
Potiphar, 20
"Potter's field," 79
Prodigal son, the, 71
Prophets, the, 7, 40-41, 53
Psalms, the book of, 7

Q-R

Queen of Sheba, 39
Rachel, 18, 20
Rahab, 28
Rainbows, 11
Rebekah, 16-17
Red Sea, 24
Resurrection of Christ, 82-83
Revelation, book of, 6, 52-53, 90-91
River Jordan, see JORDAN RIVER
Roman Empire, 53, 56, 65, 75, 87
Romans, 47, 66, 82
Rome, 88-89
Ruth, 33

S

Sabbath, the, 8, 25
Salome, 61
Samaria, 58-59, 71
Samaritans, 71, 74
Samson, 32
Samuel, 34-35
Sarah, 14
Satan, 13, 62
Saul of Tarsus, see PAUL (SAUL OF
    TARSUS)
Saul (king of Israel), 35-37
Sea of Galilee, 63, 69
Sermon on the Mount, 68
Seven seals, the, 90
Shadrach, 44
Sheba, see QUEEN OF SHEBA
Sicily, 88
Simon, see PETER
Simon (cross carrier), 80
Simon the Zealot, 64
Sinai, 25
Sisera, 29
Slaughter of the Innocents, 57
Sodom, 14-15
Solomon (king of Israel), 37-39, 44
Stephen, 87

T-U

Tabernacle, the, 26, 50
Temple, (Solomon's), 39, 44-47
Temple, the Second, 47

Temple, the Third, 47, 54, 59, 76,
    81, 86
Temple of Dagon, 27
Temptations of Christ, the, 62
Ten Commandments, 25-26
Thaddeus, 64
Thomas, 64, 84
Tower of Babel, 12
Transfiguration, the, 67
Tree of Knowledge of Good and Evil,
    8-9
Tribes of Israel, twelve, 21
Uriah, 37

W-Z

Wailing Wall, the, 47
Wedding feast in Cana, the, 66
Wise men, the three, 57
Zechariah, 54-55
Zerubbabel, 47